The Eucharist and the World of Work

The Eucharist and the World of Work

Fabio Tabori

Translated
by
Matthew J. O'Connell

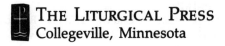
THE LITURGICAL PRESS
Collegeville, Minnesota

The Eucharist and the World of Work was originally published by Edizioni Paoline (Milan, Italy) under the title *Eucaristia e Mondo del Lavoro* © 1988 by Figlie di San Paolo.

Cover design by David Manahan, O.S.B.

Printed in the United States of America.

1	2	3	4	5	6	7	8	9

Library of Congress Cataloging-in-Publication Data

Tabori, Fabio.
   [Eucaristia e mondo del lavoro. English]
   The Eucharist and the world of work / Fabio Tabori ; translated by Matthew J. O'Connell.
     p. cm.
   Translation of: Eucaristia e mondo del lavoro.
   Includes bibliographical references.
   ISBN 0-8146-1819-7
   1. Lord's Supper—Catholic Church. 2. Work—Religious aspects—Catholic Church. 3. Catholic Church—Doctrines. I. Title.
BX2203.T3313 1990   90-35749
261.8'5—dc20   CIP

Contents

Introduction

Reflection on the presence of Christ in ourselves and in our lives, in the way we live and act, and in our daily work is a duty for which room must always be made in our daily agenda.

Our human relations and our life as members of society should be impregnated with this presence of Christ.

The short essays of this book are intended to help the reader reflect on the presence of Christ in our working lives, in that work which is so important for human beings.

The essays are not lessons in sociology, much less lectures on the subject as it applies to labor union politics. Rather they offer suggestions on various aspects of work; these suggestions may give rise to group discussion and even—why not?—group prayer. Two elements in the book may prove helpful here: the citations from the Bible and the magisterium that are offered in the several chapters, and the prayers given in the section "Suggestions for Reflection and Prayer."

I owe special thanks to those whose writings and suggestions have helped me to develop these pages.

All the rest is prayer and the hope that this tool, intended for communities and for groups ecclesial and nonecclesial, will aid in a rediscovery of the dignity of human persons, their activity in the world, and their relation to the Eucharist, which gives new meaning to that activity.

Fabio Tabori

The Eucharist and the World
of Work

1

The Eucharist, Life of the "New Human Being"

Experience of the Easter Faith

We often stop to think about our lives as Christians: how we pray and to what extent we are meaningful witnesses in today's society.

That is not enough, however. We must also bring our faith to bear on the social fabric within which we work and live our daily lives: the political order, the educational system, labor unions, the environment of work.

To belong to Christ—what a commitment, what a burden, what a laborious effort! But at the same time, what satisfaction and what interior joy spring from deep within the conviction that we belong to Christ and are the "new human beings" he looks for us to be.

Only those who experience the Easter faith and accept in their lives all the practical consequences of the event that was the death and resurrection of Christ can become "new human beings" and win the victory that has overcome the world.

For, as John Paul II has said:

> Human beings do not belong to the world; they belong to God. The resurrection of Jesus Christ has reconfirmed this basic truth about the person. The death and resurrection of Jesus were needed in order that human beings might realize the ultimate meaning of their transcendence and understand that they must "organize the world" and can (and perhaps must) "organize themselves in the world," without however surrendering to it. Human beings can trust themselves only to God, as Jesus Christ did.

"The worst despair," according to Kierkegaard, "is not to despair," and the reign of satisfied mediocrity is undoubtedly the modern expression of nihilism and perhaps even, as Bernanos suggested, of the demonic.

Today, however, it is the separation of human beings from God that seems more real and is more keenly felt. The sense of goodness, morality, and values seem to be lost or shrouded in fog or radical materialism. God is relegated to the world of fable and childish memories. God has been deleted and replaced by the idol of prosperity.

"The Church is keenly sensitive to these difficulties. Enlightened by divine revelation she can offer a solution to them by which the true state of man may be outlined, his weakness explained, in such a way that at the same time his dignity and his vocation may be perceived in their true light."[1]

The vocation of human beings is to seek the truth that has been made human and is therefore not alien to a true humanism. This truth is Jesus, the Christ.

"If we have died with him, we shall also live with him; if we endure, we shall also reign with him" (2 Tim 2:10).

Christ is therefore the pivot on which life, rebirth, and recovery turn.

Only through the concrete experience of love do "new human beings" take recognizable form: "By this all men will know that you are my disciples, if you have love for one another" (John 13:35).

There you have the Christian reality, the reality of Christ.

A Love That Spreads Throughout the World

"The dignity of man rests above all on the fact that he is called to communion with God."[2]

"All of us must endeavor to search out the plan of God that has Christ crucified and risen as its center and that overcomes the powers of hell by destroying the reign of sin and death."[3] At the Last Supper, then, Jesus made himself the bond of communion between human beings and God.

The body given and the blood shed are a gesture that manifests an infinite love.

The new meaning of the sacrifice of Jesus is conveyed by his words. While they were at table, he "took bread, and when he had given thanks, he broke it and gave it to them, saying, 'This is my body which is given for you. Do this in remembrance of me.' And likewise the cup after supper, saying, 'This cup which is poured out for you is the new covenant in my blood.'" (Luke 22:19-20). The Eucharist is thus the sacrament by means of which the Lord Jesus, crucified, risen, and alive today, makes himself constantly present among us as redeemer and continues unwearyingly to shape a new human race.[4]

The two principal means that the Church has available for carrying out its mission are the Word and the sacraments: evangelizing activity and liturgico-sacramental activity.

Word and sacrament come together and fuse in the celebration of the Eucharist. In fact, what we usually call "Christian inspiration," that is, the following of Christian moral guidelines in temporal activity, is possible only to those with courage to live their identity in its entirety and to the full.[5]

This means that we must at all times keep alive our vital links to Christ and the Church by means of the Eucharistic liturgy and therefore by coming together in a single body (see 1 Cor 11:17-20) in which the many are one in heart and soul (see Acts 4:32).

Despite all this we must admit that there are not a few negative trends abroad: the crisis of the family as an institution, the increase in abortions, the dwindling number of marriages celebrated in a religious ceremony, the problems connected with the present phase of social transformation, and— to name a few others— the introduction of new technologies in the fields of information, commu- nication, and production and the difficulty which many, especially the young and women, have in finding work.[6] In face of these strong negative trends Christians must generously make their voices heard once again in a fruitful way.

Cold statistical analysis is no longer enough, nor are pastoral letters. More is needed.

What is needed is a new evangelization of the family, society, and work. Christians must be re- born through prayer, the bread of the Word, and the Bread of Life.

It is only through the Eucharist that human beings who have been filled and transformed by the benevolence of the Father, the Son, and the Holy Spirit will become co-sources of the inex- haustible energy of love that flows out upon the world from the sacrifice of Jesus, made present to us under the signs of bread and wine.[7]

Suggestions for Reflection and Prayer

• Belonging to Christ. Only those who experience the Easter faith and accept in their lives all the practical consequences of the event that was the death and resurrection of Christ can become "new human beings" and win the victory that has overcome the world.

• The Eucharist is the sacrament in which the Lord Jesus makes himself constantly present among us and continues to form a new human race.

• Only through the concrete experience of love do "new human beings" take recognizable form: "By this all men will know that you are my disciples, if you have love for one another" (John 13:35).

Lord, our God, who has given us as spiritual food the sacrifice you offered in thanksgiving, transform us by the power and joy of your Spirit, so that we may serve you with renewed enthusiasm and once again experience your blessings.[8]

2

The Moral and Juridical Aspects of Work

Work: An Experience of the Person

A great deal has been said about the grandeur and importance of work in the life of the human person.

What, then, is "work"?

Is it simply toil, or does it embody a higher meaning? Is it simply a way of gaining a livelihood, or does it enrich the person for the good of others as well?

Work is, by definition, a product of human energies: Not only is it bathed in the sweat of the brow but it is a sign of the human person, since it always requires the intervention of the person's intellectual faculties.

> While it may seem that in the industrial process it is the machine that "works" and man merely supervises it, making it function and keeping it

going in various ways, it is also true that for this very reason industrial development provides grounds for reproposing in new ways the question of human work.

Both the original industrialization that gave rise to what is called the worker question and the subsequent industrial and postindustrial changes show in an eloquent manner that, even in the age of ever more mechanized "work," the proper subject of work continues to be man.[9]

The basis of the dignity of work is therefore human nature itself insofar as the object in view is the relationship of work to the person. Persons offer their energies to entrepreneurs, and the actual performance of work is inseparable from the person of the worker.

By comparison with machines, technology, society, and even the state, persons with all their values are themselves an absolute value and indeed the primordial value. Because of their dignity, then, workers cannot be regarded as pure objects, either in labor contracts or in the social and economic life of the nation.

As human persons, workers are the subjects of social and economic relationships and, as such, have the right to express their own thinking and to be given a hearing on their experience, whether of the organization of work or production or the economy.

Conflict arises because of an ingrained underestimation of the experience and intelligence of workers and of their contribution to the process of production.

Labor Law

The major conflicts, and the ones most likely to turn violent, are those in the area of work. As the sum total of the relationships of which work is a part grows larger and as the many sides of life in society take on more complex forms, the causes of conflict tend to be more acute and more radical.

The "person in the street," the politicians, and the workers are all involved in these conflicts and end up talking about the rights—and more rarely, the duties—of each sector.

Moreover, the various aspects of the life of work and its relationships are not discussed only by those polemically involved. They are also discussed, at the level of both abstract study and practical application, by those who feel deeply the demands of justice as this affects the world of work. These individuals like to scrutinize and, if possible, find answers to the continually renewed causes of conflict.

L. Riva Sanseverino wrote that

> the chief characteristic of "labor law," as compared with other branches of the law, whatever be the particular ordinance under discussion, is that it represents a legislative solution, reached in a particular country and at a particular time, for

the entire set of social and economic problems usually summed up as "the social question." While all law can certainly claim to be "social," the social question for which labor law provides a specific solution displays special aspects that are closely connected with a capitalist economy and are characteristic of the period that began with the French Revolution.[10]

Work understood in a juridical sense. According to Sanseverino,

in the Italian Constitution, article 1, work is described as the basis of the Italian Republic. In saying this, the Constitution intends to distance itself not only from the the political regime that preceded it but even from the economic and social context in which the Constitution came into existence and was subsequently given practical application. More particularly, the article intends to place the emphasis on the social significance of work, inasmuch as human activity tends to exert an influence outside the sphere of the one who performs it, since it is capable of producing benefits for third parties, thus giving work a specific function in relation to the result to be obtained. Article 4 refers to this same comprehensive concept of work when it identifies work as every activity or function that contributes to the material or spiritual progress of society.[11]

Work, then, is seen not as simply a means of gain but as a contribution to ends regarded as of general concern.

In regard to relations between employer and worker, the drafting of the labor contract is of primary importance, since it is this that determines the obligations of the contracting parties. A labor contract is therefore both mediator and regulator of these obligations. It binds the parties and regulates their relations at the economic level.

As Sanseverino observed, when it comes to labor contracts, the exercise of individual autonomy is undoubtedly reduced, both in our organization of things and in most other places, to a tacit acceptance by the worker of the preestablished content of the contract, which he or she agrees upon with the employer at the moment of acceptance.

Our concern here, however, is to search out the essential element. This is to be found

> in the free consent by which the relationship is established, and not in the free consent to the determination of the content of the relationship. . . . In the area of work, then, the constriction of the freedom of the parties in determining the content of the contract means a greater balance between the weight to be attached to each of the two contracting wills. From the viewpoint of society, the role of the contract is to reduce to specified, equitable forms the relations of violence and of domination by the stronger. Such a preordained organization of things limits the autonomy of the contracting parties and perfectly fulfills its social function.[12]

Labor unions play a very important role in labor contracts. They see to the exact application of the contract itself and of any union-management agreements. They suggest ways of improving methods of work. In short, they introduce into contracts an attention to the need of keeping workers informed and ensuring them a more active participation in the life and growth of the business.

When all is said and done, an increasingly practical incorporation of the workers into the running of a business should be viewed not as a likely way of heightening conflict but essentially as a form of vital collaboration between management and labor.

Solidarity and Fellowship

The element of collaboration becomes decisive, especially today when the activity of a particular company in a particular country, or even the overall economic activity of a country, can no longer be heedless of the general laws which are clearly at work in economic life.

Work, therefore, should not divide individuals but unite them.

Only by rising above individual and class self-centeredness will it be possible to achieve the common good, which is the good of all. As Leo XIII wrote, just as the symmetry of the human frame is the resultant of the disposition of the bodily members, so in a state is it ordained by nature that these two classes should dwell in harmony and agreement, and should, as it were, groove into one another, so as to maintain the balance of the body politic. Capital cannot do without labor, nor labor without capital. Harmony yields beauty and order, while perpetual conflict can only yield confusion and lead to barbarism.[13]

Therefore workers and employers "should regulate their mutual relations in a spirit of human solidarity and in accordance with the bond of Christian brotherhood. For the unregulated competition which so-called liberals espouse, or the class struggle in the Marxist sense, are utterly opposed to Christian teaching and also to the very nature of man."[14]

The Christian conception of work is the most complex and noblest possible, for it is based on the very dignity and grandeur of the intelligent, free human being who is made in God's image and is God's adoptive son or daughter.

This explains the Church's reminder, in its social teaching, of the special, profound dignity of the person and its insistence on the need of a satisfactory labor contract, a just wage, and effective support of workers in their material and spiritual needs.

But why all this? It is due, and always will be, to the fact that workers are human beings and

that their capacity for work is not to be looked
upon and treated as a mere "commodity."[15]

If people really desire and want real economic
and social progress for all, there is no other way
of achieving it than to let themselves be led by
the spirit of the gospel and illumined by its light,
which clearly distinguishes and emphasizes the
values and real needs of human nature and places
this at the center and peak of creation.

Suggestions for Reflection and Prayer

• Work is a product of human energies; it is a
sign of the human person insofar as the latter always develops by using his or her intellectual
powers. Therefore the true subject of work is, and
remains, the person, whether man or woman.
The foundation of the dignity of work is always
the person. In relation to machines, technology,
and society the person is an absolute value, the
primordial value.

• The chief characteristic of labor law is that it
represents a legislative solution, reached in a particular country and at a particular time, for the
entire set of social and economic problems usually
summed up as "the social question."

• Only by rising above personal and class self-
centeredness will it be possible to achieve the
common good and cultivate it in a spirit of
"universal solidarity and fellowship."

O God, who entrusts to every human being the daily duty of work, bless the work we are beginning, so that it will contribute to the well-being of society and the spread of your kingdom.

3

Labor Unions

Labor unions came into being as a response of workers to capitalism. Today as in the past, unions are everywhere present as a convincing proof of their usefulness as defender of the interests and aspirations of workers.

Unions represent the most concrete, widespread, and lasting answer workers have given to the conditions imposed by capitalism and to the logic at work in an economy that functions on capitalist principles.

The purpose of unions, then, is to give economic protection in several areas: work (wage level and form of wages) and the normative safeguards regulating it (holidays, work schedules); defense of jobs so as to prevent employers from acting unilaterally in their use of the work force; safeguarding the physical conditions in which workers toil (sicknesses arising from work, harmful conditions, accidents, and so on); putting pressure on the state and other institutions to secure social and economic measures that will promote the aspirations of workers, including workers on the public payroll.[16]

From the viewpoint of social morality, therefore, unionism was and is a response to

> the liberal sociopolitical system, which in accordance with its "economistic" premises strengthened and safeguarded economic initiative by the possessors of capital alone but did not pay sufficient attention to the rights of the workers, on the grounds that human work is solely an instrument of production and that capital is the basis, efficient factor, and purpose of production.[17]

Back in 1924, R. Rigola wrote:

> In order to belong to a union one need not maintain this rather than that political view, or be religious or unbelieving. It is enough that one be a worker. This is the characteristic that most clearly distinguishes a union from a political association even from one that appeals to the doctrine of class struggle. . . . The direct and specific task of a union is to improve the moral and economic conditions of workers and therefore to obtain the right kind of labor contract.[18]

Unions and the Rights of Workers

With the coming of unionism, the solidarity of its supporters produced a clearer and more effective awareness of the rights of workers and in many cases led to profound changes.

Following *Rerum Novarum* and many later documents of the Church's magisterium, we must acknowledge how justified, from the viewpoint of social morality, workers were in reacting against the harmful and unjust system that oppressed working men and women.

I shall attempt a necessarily quite general survey of union activity and of the results it produced. These results are of three kinds: material, political, and social.

The material results are the most obvious and the most widespread: the raising of salary levels against the will of employers, who thought of all wages as "subsistence wages"; the reduction of the more obvious forms of exploitation; improvements in working conditions; and the acquisition of forms of social security.

The political results are less easy to express in quantitative terms, but surely the activity of unions helped give workers more influence at the institutional political level—in securing, for example, the abrogation of laws that militated against the interests of workers and the passage of others that defended these interests (social legislation).

The social results, though perhaps less concrete, are not on that account less important or meaningful; for example, the increased esteem for work, especially manual, which led to greater equality in the working conditions of the various categories and kinds of workers. This is true especially of their treatment in law.

But the teaching of the Church is not limited to noting and applauding the results achieved. On the contrary, the magisterium has gone into and developed more fully the "moral" attitudes that should inspire unions. According to John Paul II in his encyclical on work,

> union activity undoubtedly enters the field of politics, understood as prudent concern for the common good.
>
> However, the role of unions is not to "play politics" in the sense that the expression is commonly understood today. Unions do not have the character of political parties struggling for power; they should not be subjected to the decision of political parties or have too close links with them.
>
> In fact, in such a situation they easily lose contact with their specific role, which is to secure the just rights of workers within the framework of the common good of the whole of society; instead they become an instrument used for other purposes.[19]

Nothing could be truer than these statements. In fact, we must think that the crisis of unionism and the rise of autonomous unions or other enterprises unconnected with the world of unionism are due precisely to the departure of unionism from its formative principles. I refer to the principles that made unionism the primary agent and principal exponent of the "struggle for social justice" and an "indispensable factor in social life."

Unionism should therefore continue to be "an instrument in the struggle for justice and a movement of solidarity." It must make the defense of workers' rights its chief concern, by promoting their dignity, improving their cultural and professional formation, and keeping always in mind the requirements of the common good.[20]

Suggestions for Reflection and Prayer

• Unionism exists for the economic defense of labor, its protection under law, and the protection of jobs; the prevention of a unilateral use of the work force; and the acquisition of proper working conditions.

• Unions act as political agents in the struggle for social justice and are therefore an indispensable factor in the life of society.

Be mindful, Father, of the work of your hands; grant that all of us may have job security and working conditions worthy of free men and women.

4
Employers

Relations Between Employers and Workers

Employers are no less important than employees in the workplace. For employers are those members of the work community that put their own capital into a business and thus set in motion the production of material goods.

I shall look first and foremost at the fundamental principles that must determine relations between management and labor in a business.

Starting with purely economic considerations and analyzing facts ascertainable in the living world of work, even those far removed from the Catholic or Christian faith have reached the conclusion that

> it is the task of those running a business to put into the collective operation what is best in socialism and what was best in prewar capitalism. A better life can be achieved through application of the principles of Christian ethics to the economic

order. The approach of both employers and workers must improve in accordance with a moral code governing the life of production.[21]

In the sphere of human relations, divergent views often give rise to suspicions, resentments, and open conflict between workers and employers. These disagreements show that relationships between wage earners, managers, and owners must improve at work and in life. If this improvement does not take place, the economic system will slide from crisis to crisis and never succeed in maintaining a gradual but constant improvement of the living standard and in establishing good human relationships, based on mutual respect and trust, in the life of industry and commerce.

Leo XIII said long ago that relations between workers and employers should be regulated by the principles of human, Christian solidarity.

Pius XI showed in his turn how necessary it is that the socio-economic world be rebuilt on justice and animated by social charity.

According to John XXIII, the attainment of this goal requires that

mutual relations between employers and directors on the one hand and the employees of the enterprise on the other be marked by mutual respect, esteem, and good will. It also demands that all collaborate sincerely and harmoniously in their joint undertaking, and that they perform their work not merely with the objective of deriving an income, but also of carrying out the role assigned them and of performing a service that results in benefit to others.[22]

A Business: A Community of Cooperating Individuals

Paul VI said that "a business by its very nature requires collaboration, agreement, and harmony."

A business, thus understood, must once again become a community of individuals who cooperate at the economic level and also help perfect one another at the human, moral level. This community must move toward being an integrated group, that is, one in which the members make a vital contribution by actively committing all their skills and moral gifts.

Consequently, the lower-ranking collaborators will be deeply committed to the enterprise; even more important, however, is the commitment of the entrepreneur and managers, whose behavior is often so decisive for the life of the business.

It is certainly not true that the only thing a Christian employer knows about the gospel is the parable of the talents. He finds himself living and operating in a difficult economic situation in which demand and supply follow alternating and contrary rhythms that are unbalanced; in which unemployment and the demands imposed by the restructuring of businesses create conflict; and in which the interests of profit may take second place to the concern for keeping the very business alive and productive.

The Duty of Christian Employers

In this context, Christian employers have obligations that are evidently serious. The Church speaks to this situation by its teaching, its message, and its presence.

> What we need is to know the gospel and the Scriptures generally, to stay close to them, and to see our daily life in the light of them. Why so? For two important reasons. The first is that by habit and inclination our class of people likes to get to the essential point. The second is that the vast majority of people in management have rather infantile ideas of God. . . . If there is any group that has a special need of the spiritual means which Jesus Christ has made known, it is managers. But—and here is where the crisis becomes serious—the majority of people in management who call themselves Christians rely in only a minimal degree on the means described by Christ himself. . . . Without realizing it, businessmen thus deprive themselves of a tremendous, indeed decisive help. . . . They have time for everything else, and everything else is more important, because today we no longer believe.[23]

Employers need, therefore, a spiritual and religious formation that is proportionate to the multiplicity and seriousness of the duties incumbent on them and to the personal and social impact of these duties. They need a religio-social formation that will enable them to understand social problems in their relation to the teaching of the Church. That teaching is expressed in the social encyclicals of the popes, but it must find, in the minds of Christians committed to the life of society, the further elaboration, development, and practical application that will demonstrate its validity and its intrinsic power to integrate and heal the human relationships born of industrialization.

Paul VI kept reminding and warning Christians that the social message of the Church had not been enunciated in order to remain on paper but in order to be applied. Encyclicals do not achieve their effect by themselves; they become irrelevant to the times for which they are written if, after being read and found satisfactory, they are simply put back on the shelves or are simply proposed periodically at congresses, meetings, and so on, where they assert a presence which, however, often remains theoretical.

The social teaching of the Church cannot be approached and treated in that way, for it is binding on all Christians no less than the other principles of Christian morality.[24]

John XXIII warned us:

> Let [the laity] reflect that, when in the conduct of life they do not carefully observe principles and norms laid down by the Church in social matters,

and which we ourselves reaffirm, then they are negligent in their duty and often injure the rights of others. At times, matters can come to a point where confidence in this teaching is diminished, as if it were indeed excellent but really lacks the force which the conduct of life requires.[25]

The Church, therefore, does not abandon employers or leave them isolated but rather urges them to a continual conversation in which the gospel is the other party.

The aim is to restore to business its constitutive form, which requires "collaboration, agreement, and harmony."

Paul VI exhorted Christian entrepreneurs as follows: "You are the people with dynamic ideas, the people who take salutary risks, make beneficial sacrifices, and have courageous visions: you can do great things by the power of Christian love."

Suggestions for Reflection and Prayer

• An employer is one who puts his own capital into a business and thus sets in motion the production of material goods.

• A business should be a community of people who cooperate at the economic level and seek to perfect one another at the human, moral level.

• With the aid of the Church's social teaching the entrepeneur may find himself or herself in agreement and harmony with the gospel as he or she engages in continual conversation with it.

O Lord, grant that we may not separate work from prayer but may be like St. Benedict, who took you and your apostles as his model.

5

Solidarity

The Lord Jesus in Solidarity with the Human Race

"Have this mind among yourselves, which was in Christ Jesus, who, though he was in the form of God, did not count equality with God a thing to be grasped, but emptied himself, taking the form of a servant, being born in the likeness of men" (Phil 2:5-7).

In the fullness of time, then, God sends God's own Son to establish a new covenant. The incarnation is the most obvious sign of God's solidarity with human beings. Christ becomes thereby the mediator of the new covenant.

At the Last Supper, after distributing the bread, Jesus took the cup of wine, offered the blessing over it, and said: "This is my blood of the covenant, which is poured out for many" (Mark 14:24).

The blood of Christ is not sprinkled on the altar, as in the Temple sacrifices but, together with his

body, is given to us as food. The rite expresses
the covenant that consists in the communion of
human beings with God and of brothers and sisters among themselves.[26]

God thus establishes a covenant with human
beings that frees them from slavery and helps
them bear witness in difficult times to the salvation God has wrought. A covenant of this kind
had brought the Hebrew people into a profoundly
close relationship of communion with God, but
because God is the one Father of all, the covenant also meant that all the members of the
people were obliged to live as brothers and sisters
among themselves.

This covenant God now renews in Jesus
Christ.

The human condition of enslavement, idolatry,
injustice, sin, and death is abolished by Christ,
who in the incarnation became brother to every
human being. In Christ, who loves human beings
and gives his life for them (see Gal 2:20), the Father fully reveals his solidarity with the human
race: "Jesus Christ . . . gave himself for our sins,
to deliver us from the present evil age, according
to the will of our God and Father" (Gal 1:4).

Incarnation and redemption both result from
the same movement of solidarity on Christ's part:
"Therefore he had to be made like his brethren
in every respect, so that he might become a mer-
ciful and faithful high priest in the service of God,
to make expiation for the sins of the people. For

because he himself has suffered and been tempted, he is able to help those who are tempted" (Heb 2:17-18).

Christ's priestly activity and sacrifice are acts of unlimited solidarity as Son of God and brother to other human beings. Christ is the perfect mediator; a new way has been opened (see Heb 10:18-20) whereby humanity can be raised to the level of God.[27]

The Solidarity of the Church and Christians

Solidarity in the Church is a great sea of goodness and love that embraces everyone without setting up barriers and without regard to ideology, race, and so on.

Christians cannot but take solidarity as their rule; it is a value that must inspire their every choice.

"Solidarity is the will to concretize human interdependence in relationships of collaboration and mutual support, to the benefit of all, especially the most needy." By living in solidarity, individuals overcome self-centeredness and individualism; groups overcome corporativism and exclusive party interest; nations avoid protectionism and the exploitation of other peoples.

Solidarity alone makes it possible to resolve social conflicts while respecting the demands of justice; it alone can justify personal or group renunciation in favor of the common good.[28]

The attainment of the common good is the goal set for public authorities and the political community, but all human beings can make their own contribution to its accomplishment by pursuing their private interests in ways that harmonize with the requirements of the common good according to the norms of justice.

> The true common good consists in relations of complete charity among all members of the human family. Such a condition is also in fact the full self-realization of each individual human being.
>
> Individuals can possess a great deal but be very little if they are not involved in interpersonal relationships with other human beings.
>
> The proclamation of the dogma of the Trinity leaves no room for any absolute except absolute gift. This is the final judgment that will be passed on every association and its goals.[29]

Everyday life is therefore the place where solidarity will be achieved, with the aid of the Church, which, like the gospel, preaches "the preferential option for the poor"; it is in the persons of the poor and in communion with them that our own sacrificial action takes concrete form.

The intervention of the Church (according to Msgr. Quadri) consists of formation, education, and instruction, but it also consists first and foremost of a life lived in the mystery of Christ and in communion with him.

The Church's role is therefore to proclaim and live Christ in his totality: his entire person, his entire preaching, his entire work.

This means a full acceptance of all the human and moral values found in the real Christ.

It is thus possible, through solidarity, to give an example of peaceful renewal in our own lives and in the lives of all human beings.

Suggestions for Reflection and Prayer

• God establishes with humans a covenant that frees them from slavery and supports them in trials so that they may be witnesses to salvation.

• God renews this covenant in Jesus Christ. The incarnation is the clearest sign of God's solidarity with the human race. The priestly activity and sacrifice of Christ are acts of unlimited solidarity.

• By living in solidarity Christians overcome self-centeredness and individualism; groups overcome corporativism and exclusive party interest; nations avoid protectionism and the exploitation of other peoples.

That the ecclesial community may rediscover the authentic measure of love which is the gift of self, the conquest of all selfishness, and the encounter of persons journeying together under the gaze of God: for this let us pray to the Lord.

6

The Eucharist and Work

"He who abides in me bears much fruit"

The person is thus the foundation of the dignity of work. For the person, after being created in God's image, was raised to the dignity of God's child.

By freeing the person from slavery, Christianity rehabilitates him or her and thereby restores to work its dignity and true value.

Through work human beings achieve their sanctification.

In fact, Genesis depicts God as one who works to construct the universe.

Christianity has rehabilitated work to such an extent that work, combined with prayer, has become the ideal of Christian life.

After refuting the prejudicial view that temporal activities tend to detract from the dignity of the person and believer, *Mater et Magistra* recalls the sanctifying value of work:

It is in full accord with the designs of God's providence that men develop and perfect themselves by exercise of their daily tasks, for this is the lot of practically everyone in the affairs of this mortal life.

Accordingly, the role of the Church in our day is very difficult: to reconcile this modern respect for progress with the norms of humanity and of the Gospel teaching. Yet, the times call the Church to this role; indeed, we may say, [they] earnestly beseech her, not merely to pursue the higher goals, but also to safeguard her accomplishments without harm to herself.[30]

The encyclical then proposes not only the example of Christ but a communion with him to the point where our activity is grafted on to his:

If Christians are also joined in mind and heart with the most Holy Redeemer, when they apply themselves to temporal affairs, their work in a way is a continuation of the labor of Jesus Christ himself, drawing from it strength and redemptive power: "He who abides in me, and I in him, he bears much fruit." Human labor of this kind is so exalted and ennobled that it leads men engaged in it to spiritual perfection, and can likewise contribute to the diffusion and propagation of the fruits of the Redemption to others. So also it results in the flow of that Gospel leaven, as it were, through the veins of civil society wherein we live and work.[31]

Bread and Wine, "Fruit of the Earth and the Vine"

We find the sanctification of work expressed in an exalted form in the words and rites of the sacrifice of the Mass.

There we offer bread and wine to the Lord as fruits of the earth and the vine that have acquired their present form through "the work of human hands," our work.

It is not simply the gift that God has given to us that becomes the Body and Blood of Christ. Rather, it is that gift as transformed and enriched by the work of human beings, that gift with a value added to it as a result of human work.

This work is a strict requirement, for if wheat and grapes were consecrated without first having been turned into bread and wine, the consecration would be invalid.

This shows the dignity of human work: not only the work that provides the material for the sacrifice but also the work that changes that material to make it serve the person in accordance with God's express command and, in general, all work that activates and multiplies the talents received from God.

It is usually said that "work ennobles the human being." In fact, however, it is really the converse that is true, for on reflection it is clear that "the human being ennobles work." Otherwise, the agent that does more work would be more ennobled, and human beings would be out-stripped by animals and machines.

No, it is persons who elevate the activity of animal or machine to the level of human dignity and add to a merely economic and earthly value a higher spiritual and even supernatural value, a value that transcends human and earthly limits.

Work thus loses nothing of its natural dignity but gains a higher spiritual and supernatural dignity.

Work and the sacrifice it entails are themselves redeemed and given a higher value by human beings who have been converted, healed, and renewed by the grace of the Lord's sacrifice.[32]

This offering of human work is stated once again in the Preface of the Fourth Eucharistic Prayer, prior to the consecration: "Father, we acknowledge your greatness: all your actions show your wisdom and love. You formed man in your own likeness and set him over the whole world to serve you, his creator, and to rule over all creatures."[33]

Bread and Wine, the Body and Blood of Christ

At the consecration the bread and wine that are the "work of human hands" become the Body and Blood of Christ. Christ becomes present on the altar, and we unite ourselves to his sacrifice.

Christ's words "Do this in remembrance of me" are not a simple invitation or address to the priest alone. They are a commandment to all Christians.

We are all commanded to live a genuinely Eucharistic life; to discover for ourselves the full life-giving power of God's gift; and to live out the intrinsic connection between the Eucharist and the Christian community, between the Eucharist and the Christian presence in the world.

It is this dynamic movement that brings to fulfillment the unity, the living body, the active community, and the Church of Christ.

By uniting ourselves to Christ who gave and still gives himself, we become capable of opening ourselves to others and of giving and sacrificing ourselves.

This bread and wine, then, which have been changed into the Eucharistic presence, become the food of the soul and the means of a profound communion of shared life.

The divine guest who is within us will manifest his presence in our behavior and prolong that presence into our day and our whole life.

As a result, work done under this sign of the Eucharist will recover its meaning and nobility.

Thus

> human beings, in a communion with Christ that is activated and fed by the sacrament of the altar, recover their truest dignity and identity. . . .

Fed by Christ, they already enter into the sacramental possession of eternal life and find themselves restored to the state of inviolable free creatures who are the goal of all things, all the acquisitions of science and technology, all the gains made by society. . . . The Church that celebrates the mystery of the "body given" and the "blood poured out" for each of us daily proclaims the grandeur of the human being "for whom Christ died."[34]

Suggestions for Reflection and Prayer

• In work human beings find their sanctification: "They who abide in me and I in them bear much fruit."

• The sanctification of work is carried to a higher level by the words and actions of the Mass. We present bread and wine to the Lord as "fruit of the earth/vine and work of human hands."

• "Do this in remembrance of me" is a commandment to live a genuinely Eucharistic life and to discover for ourselves all the life-giving power of God's gift.

• Work thus done under the sign of the Eucharist recovers its true meaning and nobility.

O God, who called us together for this holy Mass, which is the sign of unity and love, grant that we may trustfully carry out the work you have given to us and be able to provide the necessities of life and cooperate in the building of your kingdom.

Bibliographical Note

The literature on the social teaching of the Church is vast and is being continually updated as new documents are issued by the magisterium.

I shall mention here only a few publications that will help to a fuller understanding of the themes developed in the present book regarding the person, work, solidarity, and so on.

G. Mattei (ed.), *Il lavoro. Le encicliche sociali dalla "Rerum novarum" alla "Laborem exercens"* (Padua: Ed. Messagero).

Il discorso sociale della Chiesa. Da Leone XIII a G. Paolo II (Brescia: Ed. Queriniana).

G. B. Montini, *Al mondo del lavoro. Discorsi e scritti 1954–1963* (Brescia: Istituto Paolo VI; Rome: Ed. Studium).

J. Hoffner, *La dottrina sociale cristiana.* (Rome: Ed. Paoline).

R. Gradara, *Solidarietà e lavoro* (Rimini: Ed. Solidarieta).

Il servizio della Chiesa Italiana (= Atti Convegno "Uomini, Nuove Tecnologie, Solidarietà"; Rome: Ed. A. V. E.).

Gruppo Sacerdotale per la Pastorale del Lavoro e dell'Ufficio Liturgico Diocesano di Bologna, *Liturgia e Lavoro. Testi e documentazione* (Bologna, 1988).

Notes

1. Vatican II, Pastoral Constitution *Gaudium et Spes* on the Church in the Modern World, no. 12; trans. in Austin Flannery (ed.), *Vatican Council II. The Conciliar and Postconcilar Documents* (Collegeville: The Liturgical Press, 1975) 913.

2. *Ibid.* no. 19, 917.

3. G. Biffi, *Eucaristia, Chiesa, Mondo* (Quaderno Congresso Eucaristico Diocesano; Bologna: EDB, 1985).

4. G. Biffi, *Per la vita del mondo* (Itinerario di preparazione Congresso Eucaristico Diocesano; Bologna: Grafiche EDB, 1985).

5. S. Quadri, *L'uomo. il lavoro, la solidarietà* (Atti Convegno Regionale BO, October 14, 1984; Bologna: Centro Studi Sociali).

6. *Il Papa a Loreto, Discorsi ai partecipanti al Convegno della Chiesa Italiana*, 1985.

7. G. Biffi, *Eucaristia* (n. 3) 60.

8. The prayers at the end of each chapter are from the collection *Liturgia e lavoro* (see Bibliographical Note).

9. John Paul II, *Laborem Exercens* on Human Work, no. 5, translated in *Origins* 11 (1081–82) 229.

10. L. Riva Sanseverino, *Il diritto del lavoro*, 3–4.

11. *Ibid.* 31–35.

12. *Ibid.* 125.

13. Leo XIII, *Rerum Novarum,* no. 13.

14. John XXIII, *Mater et Magistra,* no. 23, trans. in J. Gremillion (ed.), *The Gospel of Peace and Justice. Catholic Social Teaching Since John XXIII* (Maryknoll, N. Y.: Orbis Books, 1976) 148.

15. *See* Pius XII, Address to the Workers of the Fiat Corporation, 1948.

16. *See A cosa serve il Sindicato?,* I, 7.

17. *See Laborem Exercens,* no. 8.

18. R. Rigola, *Manualetto di tecnica sindicale* (1947).

19. *Laborem Exercens,* no. 20 *(Origins,* 239).

20. R. Gradara, *Solidarietà e lavoro* (Rimini: Ed. Solidarieta).

21. R. W. Johnson, *Relazioni umane nell'impresa moderna* (New York, 1949).

22. *Mater et Magistra,* no. 92, 163.

23. B. Sassoli De Bianchi, *Appunti de "Integrazione dell'uomo nell'azienda"* (Ucid E. R.).

24. *See Osservatore Romano,* June 1964.

25. *Mater et Magistra,* no. 241, 194.

26. *See* Gradara (n. 20), 49.

27. *Ibid.* 50–51.

28. *Ibid.* 88.

29. E. Chiavacci, *Principi di morale sociale,* 30–31.

30. *Mater et Magistra,* no. 256, 197.

31. *Ibid.* no. 259, 198.

32. *See* U. Tomarelli, *La mia Messa* (Rome, 1975).

33. Fourth Eucharistic Prayer in the Sacramentary of the Roman Missal.

34. Biffi, *Eucaristia* (n. 3) 60.

Notes